MARK OEST...
& BROCK M...

A

PARENT'S GUIDE

TO UNDERSTANDING

TEENAGE GUYS

REMEMBERING WHO HE WAS,
CELEBRATING WHO HE'S BECOMING

simply for parents

A Parent's Guide to Understanding Teenage Guys
Remembering Who He Was, Celebrating Who He's Becoming

© 2012 Mark Oestreicher and Brock Morgan

group.com
simplyyouthministry.com

Credits
Authors: Mark Oestreicher and Brock Morgan
Executive Developer: Nadim Najm
Chief Creative Officer: Joani Schultz
Copy Editor: Rob Cunningham
Cover Art and Production: Veronica Preston

Scripture quotations marked NIV are taken from *THE HOLY BIBLE*, NEW INTERNATIONAL VERSION®, NIV® Copyright © 1973, 1978, 1984, 2011 by Biblica, Inc.™ Used by permission. All rights reserved worldwide.

ISBN 978-0-7644-8459-9

10 9 8 7 6 5 4 3   20 19 18 17 16 15 14 13

Printed in the United States of America.

CONTENTS

INTRODUCTION

Let's start with this: Long before each of us was a youth worker (combined, we've been youth workers for more than 50 years!), both of us were teenage guys. And because we spend so much of our time with teenagers, we've worked hard to remember what it was like to actually *be* a teenage guy.

I (Brock) remember getting that dreaded phone call. It was about 6 o'clock on a Saturday evening, and I had spent the previous night at my friend's house with the understanding that I would call my dad first thing in the morning. All day had passed, and it was now beginning to get dark. Throughout the day I had occasionally thought about calling him, but then I'd quickly get distracted with adolescent adventure. It all came crashing down when my friend's mom came out to the front yard where we were horsing around and said, "Brock, your dad is on the phone." I felt instant panic. You know, the pit-in-the-stomach syndrome that comes when you know that you are about to die. I walked toward that 1980s avocado green phone with the long curly cord and tried to quickly think of excuses for why I disobeyed my dad. "Hello?" I said. "Brock, come home right now; you are in big trouble." "But, Dad!" "Big trouble, Brock."

I (Marko) had so many of these moments, it's difficult to pick one. But I will absolutely never forget the moment in the mall parking lot. I'd just totaled one of the family cars on my first driving date, a week after getting my driver's license. The mall parking lot was empty except for the sad wreckage of our family VW Bug. I thought my older sister was coming to pick up my date and me. And I thought it would be funny to jump around like a clown on crack, clarifying the location of the obvious carnage. But when the ride home pulled up, it was my dad. Though only about 30 minutes, that was the longest drive home I ever had with my dad.

Our parents tell us that during our adolescence, they regularly felt worried and would lose sleep over us. At times they felt out of their depth as they tried to graciously guide us through dating relationships, school grades, teenage temptation of all sorts, knucklehead choices, teenage experimentation, and our spiritual lives.

We each remember the worried expressions on their faces, as neither of us seemed to think before we acted.

We remember feeling powerless in making good choices and wanting them to rescue us, while at the same time *not* wanting them to rescue us.

We remember being conflicted and double-minded.

We remember the feeling of overwhelming regret when we failed to listen to our parents.

We remember confessing stupidity or sharing deep pain, and we remember the hurt we saw in their eyes—and how they still lovingly responded to us.

These were not easy years.

We are writing this book as sons, as youth workers of multiple decades, and as parents of teenagers ourselves (Brock has a 15-year-old daughter and has been the legal guardian of a now 19-year-old, and Marko has an 18-year-old daughter and a 14-year-old son). We know that the journey for teenage guys is one of failure and triumph, of defeat and victory, of joy and sorrow—and we hope that our personal experience brings texture to our stories and insights. Our prayer is that this little book will help you along the way.

We pray that all of you will see your sons with the eyes of Jesus and that, through you and others, they will begin to capture the dream of God for their own lives.

CHAPTER 1: SHEPHERDING AT HOME IN A SHIFTING CULTURE

Because both of us are youth pastors, we've often approached parenting teenagers from that perspective. My wife (Marko here), when we're in a challenging conversation about how to respond to a tough parenting spot, often says, "Put your youth pastor hat on; what would you say to yourself as a parent?"

When I (Brock) was first parenting, I regularly felt out of my depth. I was learning how to be an effective pastor of students, though, and one day I experienced this moment of revelation: "I can just be a youth pastor at home!" As youth workers we're intentional about creating environments of growth—environments where students grow closer to each other, grow closer to caring adults, and grow closer to God. I thought, "Well, that sounds like a great way to parent. I'll just do that. As a family we'll do activities that help us grow closer to each other and closer to the Lord. I'll just pastor at home."

Pastoring or shepherding at home means we have to be strategic, engaged, and prayerful. We have to be aware of what's going on in the home and in the lives of our family members. We have to strategically create environments where they can experience the warmth of God. In a world where culture could literally destroy, or at the very least distract and sidetrack our families (and ourselves), we have to be purposeful as parents. We want our children to know that they're never alone, that we're here for each other. And ultimately, we long for them to discover the God who has always been there with them, since before they were born.

One of the most important roles of a shepherd is to know the environment and the terrain. To shepherd, you've got to know the land the sheep are living in.

It's Not the Same World

As youth workers, we are constantly reminded that the teenage landscape is a very different world than it was when we were teenagers. We have even found that what was effective with students 10 years ago doesn't work nearly as well today. The mindset of today's teenager is different, and multiple factors contribute to this reality.

This first factor is that students are growing up in a *culture of immediacy*. Think about it: When you were a kid, you went to the library to do research for your report. It could take you all day to gather the information. Today, students can get any information they want within seconds. They can text a friend, touch base with Mom, and turn in a paper all at the same time, with just the push of a button.

I (Brock) remember getting separated from my mom at the mall when I was a boy, and I thought I was lost for good. I had to wait for her to find me in the security area, hoping soon that she'd realize I wasn't with her. I sometimes think she viewed the security of the malls in our area as free child care. But today, you just use your cell phone and abracadabra, you're found. No waiting necessary.

But how, in this culture of immediacy, can your son's faith grow when Scripture tells us to be still, and to be quiet and wait on the Lord? No wonder teenage guys are leaving the faith for seemingly easy and immediate fixes.

Statistics on teenagers' use of technology

- One in three send over 100 text messages per day (March 2012, Pew Report)
  pewtrusts.org/our_work_detail.aspx?id=56

- 93 percent of teenagers go online daily (Pew Report 2010) *pewinternet.org/Reports/2010/Social-Media-and-Young-Adults.aspx*

- The average teenage boy watches 50 pornographic videos per week (TED Talks, the demise of guys) *blog.ted.com/2011/08/05/talk-and-survey-are-we-seeing-the-demise-of-guys-philip-zimbardo-on-ted-com/*

Another difference of youth culture today: Teenagers are *way too busy and far too overscheduled.* Today's students have no time unfilled. Their day begins at 5 a.m. and often doesn't end until after midnight. They might play on multiple sports teams at once while taking college prep courses and working 20 hours a week at a part-time job. They are beyond busy and can't imagine being anything else. All the while, their parents applaud this pace of life and view it as a way to keep their son out of trouble or to build the college résumé.

T.S. Elliot once wrote that we are "distracted from distraction by distraction" (*Four Quarters*, Mariner Books, 1968). And Oswald Chambers writes in *My Utmost for His Highest* (Oswald Chambers Publications, 1992), "The greatest enemy of a life of faith is not sin, but good choices which are not quite good enough. The good is always the enemy of the best."

In places like Florida and Arizona, seasonal senior citizens are called snowbirds. Church youth groups around the country have "seasonal" teenagers. These are students who disappear from youth group depending on the season: band season, soccer season, SAT season. You get the picture. This has a huge impact on our sons, and we hear every week that their biggest struggle in following God is that they just don't have the time. What are we doing?

Adults might think that teenagers' lives are carefree and full of free time. However, a recent KidsHealth® KidsPoll shows that students have quite a different opinion. Of the 882 students ages 9 to 13 that were polled, 41 percent reported feeling stressed most of the time or *always*, because they have too much to do (February 2012 - kidshealth.org/kid/talk/kidssay/poll_stress.html#).

Another compounding reality for teenage guys is that they've grown up in a culture where *everything is disposable*. Their phones, cameras, water bottles, and even relationships are disposable. When we were in middle school and fell in love with a cute girl with big bangs, we actually thought about what it would be like to marry her. Many of today's teenagers enter relationships knowing full well that they won't last.

Temporary and disposable are the norm. This mindset of disposability even creeps into faith. If everything in the world is disposable, why not a faith that's "disposable" if it's not working for me this week?

An obvious aspect of our culture that is also having a major impact is *the sexualization of all things*. It's not like kids weren't horny when we were growing up, of course. But the cultural landscape of sexuality continues to expand and change. This is having profound impact on our guys *and* our girls. Watch the ads during the Super Bowl, and you see what our culture is telling teenagers they should value. Every commercial seemingly falls into one of a few categories: Sex, Beer and Sex, or Cars and Sex.

When we were kids growing up, pornography wasn't very accessible. The first time either of us ever saw a Playboy® magazine (which, if we're honest, is tame compared to online porn), we were in middle school. We both still remember that first sighting. I (Brock) was playing war with my friends in the woods and just happened to stumble upon a magazine. I (Marko) was in the backyard shed of a wild kid in my neighborhood, who'd stolen a magazine from his dad. Today, many sixth- and seventh-grade guys are already addicted to Internet porn.

It's just a different world, and the accessibility to porn is almost omnipresent and creeps into the lives of nearly every teenage guy. And this reality absolutely has an impact on their everyday lives. I (Brock) took a break from writing this section to hang out with a 15-year-old guy in my youth group. He confessed to hooking up (having casual sex) with random girls, girls he didn't even know. I just spoke to a youth worker in Texas who told me that the *student leaders* in her youth group were caught playing a game in a back room at the church where every student put money in a jar, and the two girls who were willing to make out with each other in front of the group got to split the cash.

Mainstream media, heavily influenced by pornography, normalize this kind of behavior. The more we see something, the more ordinary it becomes. It's no longer shocking. This is having a profound impact, one we'll dive into a little deeper later in this book.

One more shaping cultural factor we'll mention in this chapter is that today's teenage guys have grown up in a culture with a *"Starbucks® spirituality."* Teenagers personalize and customize their faith like ordering a drink at Starbucks: "I'll have a kabbalah latte, with a shot of Buddhism, some Jesus on top, and a Krishna cookie on the side." The guys in our small groups have no problem with contradiction. One "truth" doesn't have to exactly fit with another "truth." This is a complex issue for sure, but as parents, are we graciously guiding them through this culture?

Last year I (Brock) was away with our high school group for a weekend retreat. On Saturday night I spoke, we all worshipped, and God moved. Students all over the room were repenting of their rebellion, giving their lives to Jesus, and praying for each other. It was one of those nights that keeps me in youth ministry and makes me think that all the investment is finally paying off. Afterward I was sitting with a group of 10th-grade guys, and they were all sharing what Jesus had done in their hearts. Then John spoke up: "Tonight God told me that reincarnation is true." I, along with everyone present, looked at him, wondering if he was joking. But then we realized, "He's serious!" Thank goodness, his buddy cut through the awkwardness and came to the rescue with, "Dude, wrong religion."

Many students have no problem taking portions of other religions and applying the parts that resonate. As youth workers and parents in this culture, we're often reminded of the early church. And we have to graciously be our sons' guides. We can't be afraid that they'll choose poorly or get off the path of Jesus. We must trust the Lord and not parent out of fear. We have to remind ourselves that Scripture will not return void or be taught to them in vain.

And we must also allow them to teach us. In many situations we need to be both a listener and a learner. We have to help guide them toward the ultimate big-T Truth. This openhanded approach actually helps young men become critical thinkers and opens their eyes to see how significant a life of faith is in the midst of a very complex world.

I (Brock) have to finish the story of the "reincarnation guy." He came to another camp a few months later. He never once felt condemned by our group or by me. And on a summer night, on top of a houseboat, he gave his life to Jesus. I could have squashed him prior to that night, but I decided to trust that God was at work in his life, that God would reveal himself in due time.

CHAPTER 2:
THE EXTREME STRUGGLES
OF TEENAGE GUYS

Isolation

One evening Dave came right up to the stage after I (Brock) closed in prayer. With tears in his eyes he said, "Brock, I think it's time you hear my story." I was surprised because Dave seemed like he had it all together. He was good looking, a great athlete, smart, and popular. He was a natural leader and was passionate about life. But he began to tell me the painful narrative of his life and how his father had abandoned his family. He talked about his parents' divorce and how before his father left, he took Dave out for a drive around the neighborhood. As they were driving around, his dad began to tell Dave the divorce was Dave's fault. His father looked at him and said, "I wish you'd never been born." Sitting in that family car with his dad, Dave began to cry so hard that his nose started bleeding all over the front of his shirt and onto the car upholstery.

At this point in the story Dave looked at me and said, "My dad then stopped in front of our house and let me out. That's the last time I ever spoke to him." He continued, "Brock, I'm not making it in life. I feel myself becoming angry like my dad. I need help. And I was just wondering if you would be my father?" What a question. What an honor.

Dave's story is less uncommon than you might think. Actually, the only thing truly uncommon about Dave's story is that he reached out for help, rather than continuing in his loneliness. What we've seen in hundreds, even thousands of teenage guys, is that even those from what *appear* to be solid, two-parent, churchgoing homes are struggling with loneliness at an alarming rate. Teenage girls also struggle with this in our culture, but in many ways, it's a distinctly *male* issue.

We all know that it's not supposed to be like this. But how we respond as parents—even if we can't solve all their friendship (or lack of friendship) problems—can teach our sons that they are loved, safe, supported, and believed in. Dave's story might be a little extreme, and his story may not be yours or your son's, but there's zero hesitation for us in telling you that the majority of teenage guys, at some point, feel isolated.

As their children head into the teen years, most parents tend to withdraw a bit. They stop shepherding at home.

They may not abandon their family like Dave's dad did, but they definitely tend to take a step back, becoming a little bit more passive and disengaged in their parenting role. Maybe we as parents just grow weary of the battles of rebellion, or maybe we just feel overwhelmed when it comes to the challenge of parenting adolescent sons. And some of these guys do look like men. But don't be fooled: Until the late teen years, each one really is a boy in a man's body, all alone, making his way through this crazy world.

Research can help us on this issue. For his book *Guyland* (Harper Collins, 2008), Michael Kimmel interviewed more than 400 adolescent boys. Kimmel says that most teenage guys feel utterly alone as they chart their path through the world. By the time guys hit high school, they feel like they can't trust their parents or other adults—and most feel like they can't trust each other either. Kimmel attributes this to the "guy code" that prescribes, "Boys don't cry, boys don't show emotion, and boys definitely are never to be vulnerable." Guys spend significant effort trying to prove that they aren't like girls and that they are masculine enough to warrant independence in the "real man's" territory.

In other words, guys have closed themselves off because they don't feel safe to just be themselves. They are spending their high school years detached, because every time they express emotion, other than anger, they feel vulnerable and face ridicule. Now, here's the catch: They are longing to be set free from this, but at the same time, they don't think it's possible. They are stuck, which leads to a hidden existence, constantly withdrawing from their true selves.

As we try to engage in the lives of our sons, we must help them develop a true sense of self, not pull away, not put up walls of defense, not isolate. And as parents, we can make a difference; we can rescue our sons from a disengaged, lonely existence.

First know this: **Every teenage guy needs a dedicated fan.** You need to be his No. 1 fan. But he also really needs someone outside of the family who will be there for him through life's ups and downs, joys and sorrows. Because of teen issues of feeling isolated and all alone, he needs someone who will listen to him and gently speak truth in love.

Who, besides you, is regularly investing in your son? Back in the day it was enough to have a coach or a teacher take an interest in our children. But with culture shifting so dramatically, parents can't assume that the mere presence of another adult in the life of their son will provide this safe and encouraging relationship. It's becoming more and more important to have God-honoring men investing in our sons, men who are carving a pathway for them to follow. They need men who love deeply and are living the way of Jesus—bringing the light of Jesus into the dark places of this world. They need men who don't just talk about faith but are actually living it. Teenage guys are drawn to action, but faith often seems so passive and legalistic to them. God-honoring "action heroes" are needed, and parents have to be intentional about fostering and hosting those relationships.

This isn't about abdicating your own presence. You as a parent must stay connected and help usher your son into manhood. There will come a time, if it hasn't happened already, when your son will try to pull away. This is the normal process of individuation, the process of moving from childhood into adulthood. In order to become their own person, most adolescents, for a time, pull away from their parents' ideas, values, and perspectives.

When someone is actively pulling away from you, it's natural to slip into one of two extremes: Either you force that person to stay, or you passively let that person go. When parenting teenage guys, both responses are harmful.

Unfortunately, as youth workers, we see both responses all of the time.

Every teenage guy needs measured freedom. We've heard it said that parenting teenagers is like flying a kite. Your children enter their teen years and you, as a parent, must slowly let the line out. You've been teaching them how to fly, and now it's time to practice a bit. As you let the line out, you're focusing on the conditions and the environment the kite is flying in. Sometimes you let the line go way out, watching carefully but allowing them to ride the wind. Because of your own experience, you know the winds change, so sometimes you have to gently pull the kite back in close. In order for you to know when to pull the kite back, you have to be keenly aware of what's needed for this little kite to make it.

We love this picture, because to fly a kite, you must be always watching, always aware, always engaged. If you take your eye off the kite, it might end up in a tree or crash to the ground! Please don't take a back seat in your son's life; stay thoughtfully engaged.

Next, **every teenage guy needs a passion or interest area in which he can develop competence.** For example, we are always looking for young musicians to put in the worship band at our churches or tech guys to help run the media (Marko's son, Max, finds a great sense of competency in being the drummer for the middle school band at our church).

What competencies do you see in your son? What is he drawn to, and how can you help him develop and grow in that ability? What flicker of interest do you see in your son, and how might you help his passion become a skill?

Lastly, **every teenage guy needs real, enduring friendship.** Guys need at least one other guy friend to help them think critically about the direction the crowd is going. We love Philippians 2. It talks about being deep-spirited friends, something we all need and something teenagers are desperate to have. My mom (Brock here) used to tell me that my friends were a mirror reflection of my heart. I hated it when she said it, but it actually made me think through my friend choices. Honestly, over the past 22 years of youth ministry, I've seen this played out over and over again. The friends we choose can reveal something about ourselves.

As a parent you can feel a bit powerless in the friends your children choose. But it reveals something important and something vital about our children's hearts. What people are they drawn to? This is another reason why youth group is just so vital. We like to call it the great reversal. Students often attend a school where they think no one believes in God, but then they come into our youth room and see students who are engaged in the faith. They see students who aren't perfect but are part of something bigger than themselves, students who have invited adults into their lives to help shepherd them through life's challenges. As parents, we want our children to have friends in their lives who are wide-open to Jesus and his followers.

Anger

Growing up I (Brock) had a really difficult time with anger. I'd get in a fight with my older sister and end up hitting her or punching a hole in the wall. Out of frustration with me, my dad advised, "Listen, Brock, if you need to hit something, go hit your bed!" So I used to go and beat the snot out of that bed. But honestly, this was a little weird, so my dad thought of a better idea. He told me that when I got really upset, I should do something productive and use this adrenaline of anger for good. He'd have me exercise, mow the lawn, or just go out for a run. So I was in really good shape during my teen years, and our lawn was the envy of the neighborhood. Teenage guys struggle with anger, and they *feel* strongly.

When you're trying to help your son with his anger, it's important to first remember that anger is not always a bad thing. We all know about the time Jesus was so upset he started throwing tables around the temple courtyard. Not that we want our sons to mimic that particular example in our homes, but there is a time for anger. Sometimes things happen that are wrong or unjust and require an appropriate amount of anger. Don't rush to squash your son's anger; instead, try to help him understand it. The only rule we would encourage is that in our anger, we don't dishonor, disrespect, or hurt people.

And we need to be careful because anger is contagious and can suck you in. In the midst of an angry interaction, take a step back; give your son some space. Then, after some time, re-engage and talk with him about it. When a son starts yelling, parents often yell back. In the end this will make your son feel unsafe, unwanted, and disrespected. Treat him like you'd want to be treated. Most teenage guys don't have role models in their lives who can help them articulate the dynamite that's getting ready to explode inside of them. Nor do many guys have the ability to verbalize and work through the issues that are troubling them like most girls can. It's our job as parents to help our sons, after a cooling-down time, to verbally process and discover what's really going on.

When talking with your son, look for the kernel of truth behind his anger. Affirm that truth and say something like, "Oh, that makes sense; can you tell me more about that?" This will legitimize the feeling and help him pinpoint why he's experiencing such emotion. Give your son some freedom to express himself a bit, while gently reminding him of the rule of not dishonoring or disrespecting.

Of course, in the midst of a power struggle with your son, sometimes you're going to have to say no to something that he wants. Try not to do this without first having dialogue. He may not come to an agreement with you, but you will have calmly explained yourself and given him a vision for your reasoning.

Lust

Addiction has gone mainstream. The TV show *Celebrity Rehab* presents pop personalities checking in and Dr. Drew trying to help them wade through their world of dysfunction and brokenness, all for the audience's entertainment. Go to a grocery store and glance at the magazines near the checkout: The covers are full of addiction, excess, and overindulgence. Teenage guys have always struggled with lust; that's nothing new. But in today's culture, there's almost a sense where you don't have a real life story unless addiction has played prominently. And never has an addiction been more in-your-face for such a large percentage of teenage boys than pornography is today.

Recently a few ninth-grade guys and I (Brock) were hanging out and the topic of porn came up. Every single one of them was struggling with pornography on a daily basis. I asked them if their parents let them take their laptop into their room and if they even had a filter or any accountability software on their computers. I really shouldn't have been surprised when one of them said, "Why would they do that? My dad looks at porn every day!" Before you shake your head in disgust at *that dad*, remember the others in the group: They were *all* struggling.

The more you see something, the more it gets normalized. Porn is quickly becoming normalized in our culture, and it's starting to be viewed as ridiculous to guard against it. But here's the deal: These ninth-grade boys were *miserable* and wanted someone to rescue them. They actually wanted their parents to put a filter on their computer so that if they went to a "bad" website, their parents would be made aware. They actually wanted their cell phones to *not* have Internet access. One student told me that his mom had recently caught him looking at porn. He told me that it was the best thing because for once he felt hope in this area.

Of course, at the same time, they wanted their parents to leave them alone. They are, in a word, conflicted. Our guys are confused, and we as parents must engage them on this subject. (By the way: Saying one time, "Don't look at porn," is not engagement.)

A new study shows that 12- to 14-year-olds exposed to the most sexual content in movies, music, magazines, and on television were 2.2 times more likely to have had sexual intercourse when reinterviewed two years later than their peers who had a lighter sexual media diet. Sexual entertainment = sexual teenagers.

Many of our guys are falling into these traps because they believe that "everyone is doing it." But the truth is that not everyone is doing it. The National Center for Health Statistics recently reported research on teen sexual activity. Researchers found that 53 percent of 15- to 17-year-old boys and 58 percent of 15- to 17-year-old girls have never had a sexual encounter. And when you isolate the data to just 15-year-olds, 64 percent report no sexual experience with another person. This is good news and something we'd like to build upon. The reality is that other research tells us that boys are not honest about their responses on self-reporting tests, leading to highly inflated numbers for sexual activity. In the locker room they can talk a pretty big game, which contributes to the mindset that all of their friends are sexually active. As parents, we can set the record straight and, more importantly, give them a vision for a better way.

Although the study showed that one of the biggest risk factors for early teen sex was the perception that a teenager's friends were having sex, researchers say one of the strongest *protective* factors was the parental attitude about sex (National Health Statistics Reports, Number 36, March 3, 2011).

This is good news, by the way. Your views about these issues matter. But we want to caution you: It's vital that you're wise in how you communicate your views. It's important to appeal to your son's heart, giving him a vision for who he really is, and it's best to start this when he's young. You have the power to help your son see women as sacred, view themselves as sacred, and choose to live a life of integrity and respect.

Some of you reading this might be thinking, "But I totally messed up myself when I was that age!" We both love the movie *The Shawshank Redemption*. Morgan Freeman plays a man who has served 40 years of a life sentence. Toward the end of the movie he's sitting before the parole board, whose members want to know why they should let him go free. He looks at them and says, "There's not a day that goes by that I don't feel regret over what I did. I look back on the way I was then, a young stupid kid who committed that terrible crime. And I want to talk to him. I want to try and talk some sense to him. Tell him the way things are. But I can't. That kid is long gone, and this old man is all that's left."

As parents and youth workers, we pull out the *Shawshank* speech every now and again. It's a good one to have in your tool kit. We say things like, "I made mistakes, choices that didn't just impact me but everyone around me. And I want to tell my 15-year-old self not to go down that road— but I can't. What I can do is tell you. I want a better life for you. I want you to experience an amazing life lived without the heaviness that bad decisions bring."

Hurt

Today's teenagers are living with a heightened amount of hurt and pain. They're cutting and burning themselves, dealing with eating disorders and depression, and feeling isolated and alone (abandoned, some would say) in a very confusing world. They're growing up in a world that is not carefully guiding them into maturity, and—honestly—has very little expectation of them. As parents it's easy to dismiss the pain our children are carrying or just to cross our fingers and hope it's not a big deal.

We've both heard, countless times, from parents who tell us their son is doing fine with the fact that they're divorcing. But we hear a very different story at youth group. It's just that their son wasn't communicating with his parents and was too afraid to ask questions that got beneath the surface.

This isn't just a divorce issue, by the way. It's merely an example we're offering. In our experience, *most teenagers* are carrying some amount of pain and hurt, and they *all* experience it profoundly at times.

In his book *Hurt*, Chap Clark says, "We have evolved to the point where we believe driving [our teenagers] in a car somewhere is support, being active is love, and providing any and every opportunity is selfless nurture. We are a culture that has forgotten how to be together. We have lost the ability to spend unstructured downtime." We have abandoned them to institutions, to busyness, to our need as adults to feel good about ourselves.

Over our years in youth ministry, we have seen many girls who had eating disorders. But over the last 10 years we have, for the first time, witnessed many teenage guys in our youth groups develop eating disorders, too. The world they are growing up in is killing them on the inside, and as parents we can't just hope they get through it. It may not be an eating disorder, but we have to be sensitive and thoughtful in how we are coming alongside our children.

Here are some signs to watch for that might indicate your son is struggling with hurt:

- Withdrawal; avoiding people

- Negative attitude

- Mood changes

- Apathy: "I don't care"

- Taking things personally; being overly sensitive to innocent comments

- Possessiveness; being unnecessarily jealous

- Critical and demanding attitude

- Inability to forgive, even the "little" things

- Confused, especially by other people and
  their actions

And here are some quick thoughts about how you might
help him through his pain:

- Help him identify what's really going on. Ask
  questions that will get to the root issue(s).

- Help him talk about ways of forgiving. Don't
  force him to forgive. The two of you talking about
  forgiveness helps prepare him to be ready and able
  to forgive at the appropriate time.

- Help him decide if he needs to talk to the person
  who hurt him. Help him know how to confront
  a wrong without being reactionary and overly
  confrontational.

- Help him rediscover who loves him. Identify ways
  family and friends show him love. Many teenagers
  are longing for perfect, unconditional love. Help him
  learn to accept imperfect love from other people.

- Guard against too much mistrust. When teenagers repeatedly experience hurt, they simply stop trusting everybody.

- Set up an appointment with a counselor who can help your son talk through what's going on inside. This is not a last-case scenario. We should get in the habit of pursuing tuneups in life, and talking with a counselor can help us think through life's struggles and difficulties.

Apathy

On a recent Saturday, after realizing he had already watched a few hours of TV, I (Marko) asked my teenage son, "What do you want to do this weekend?" "I don't know." "Do you want to get together with some friends? Or play your drums? Or do something outside?" "Not really."

I temporarily gave up, not wanting to fight him on it. But later that night, when he started complaining about what a *boring* day it had been, I wished I'd offered options a bit better. Not that it's my job to keep my son entertained, but I want to come alongside him and help him push through the natural apathy he often faces.

Many teenage guys walk around the hallways of their schools, their homes, and their churches like zombies. They're afraid to show too much emotion, afraid of risk that might result in embarrassing failure. They perceive men as being like Arnold Schwarzenegger's Terminator: unmoved, unemotional, only uttering phrases like "I'll be back."

Teen guys believe they need to protect themselves because they feel vulnerable; all of these newfound emotions are bubbling just below the surface. We've learned as youth workers that some of the most passionate students in our groups are the ones who are walking with numb expressions on their faces.

They are passionate about friends, family, schoolwork, sports, their faith, and the world. But occasionally, if one area in life isn't going well, they'll throw up the walls and act like they don't care. What this can reveal, if you dig a bit, is that they actually care more than you thought. They care enough to convince themselves and you that they don't. For example, I (Brock) had a seemingly apathetic and overly busy 10th-grade guy who was finally moved by God on the last day of a mission trip. He grew teary-eyed and prayed with me, but found it hard to express what had just happened to him; he just knew that God was with him, and he was overwhelmed. Two months passed with me hardly seeing him, and when I did, he appeared emotionally detached. But then I got a text message asking to meet. We met for three and a half hours and I could hardly get a word in. He had dozens of great questions about faith, and at the end of our time together, he told me that that he thought God wanted him to be a youth pastor. Go figure.

Your son really cares. He might be afraid to show it, but trust us—he has deep emotions that are just below the surface.

The Pull of the Virtual World

"Pac-Man®," "Galaga®," "Frogger®"—nope, today's games are not like ours were.

Video games today are a world apart from the ones most of us played as teenagers. (Marko here: Brock might have played "Pac-Man" and "Frogger," but my era was a bit more "Pong.") Today's games involve interacting virtually with fellow gamers around the world. Modern virtual reality games are like ancient Greek epics in which everyone gets to feel like Aeneas or Odysseus. Games today are really fun but can be all-consuming. Some gamers tend to completely give up reality for their virtual worlds. Video game addictions, especially among teenagers and twentysomethings, are common story lines. I (Brock) had a high school guy in my youth group who actually started skipping school and ended up not graduating because of his gaming addiction.

But what do we do about this as parents?

First, boundaries need to be clear. For example, no gaming until homework and chores are completely done. You might even want to set a time limit as well, particularly when your son is playing by himself. In our home (Marko), we have a "screen time" limit that includes computers, TV, phones, and any other screen my kids can think up. Our "screen time" limit on school nights is 30 minutes for my middle school son and one hour for my high school daughter (and only if homework is completed).

Another aspect to the gaming world is that it can easily replace true living. Adventure in the games replaces real-life adventure. Be intentional as a family to regularly and habitually get out of the house for hikes, climbs, runs, and explorations. Even restaurant exploration or an old-fashioned game of bowling can do the trick. Don't let your teenage son forget how to live. In fact, put on your family calendar a monthly adventure where you are paddleboarding, canoeing, or traversing a terrain together, surrounding yourself with creation and fresh air.

A third aspect to all of this is monitoring and protecting your home. The values and ethics that are taught in the virtual world can be toxic and deadly to a spiritual life. We recommend installing on all of your family's computers, including your own, a filter or reporting software that will email you where everyone has been online (xxxchurch. com has free software that will email browsing results—be honest with your son that you're installing this).

With all these "extreme struggles of guys," we parents have to get out in front and beat culture to the punch. If you can set parameters early, your parenting will be so much easier. If you're starting a little late, don't lose hope. Have a family meeting, appeal to your son's heart, give him vision, and empower him to help set the family's guidelines.

CHAPTER 3: PREPARING HIM TO TAKE THE REINS

There are so many guys masquerading as men today, boys who never grew up. They have careers and nice cars, but they have no discipline and no vision for why God has placed them here on earth. They are little man-boys in adult clothing. They do what they want, when they want, and they're living a shallow story. But that's not going to be your son's story, right? Boys were meant to grow into men, men who join and contribute to the greatest story—the story of freedom and life that God has called us all to join.

We've found that young men today are dying for a life worth living. They want to be a part of something bigger than themselves, and they often aren't finding that story in the church. They're just told by the church what *not* to do. And that seems kind of boring. But what if the gospel was dangerous and required everything? What if it meant denying yourself, picking up your cross, and following Jesus (Luke 9:23)? What if it was about bringing light to dark places, being a part of redeeming tragedy, and bringing justice?

When I (Brock) was 13, my parents took my older sister
and me to Haiti. It was in the mid-'80s and there were
riots happening all over the country because of a corrupt
election. We were there for about 14 days working in
orphanages, feeding people, and working the land to
help crops grow in a village. Toward the end of our trip,
I remember standing on the side of a street in Port-Au-
Prince, feeling frightened by the mobs of screaming people.
I was standing next to my dad, and I looked at him and
asked, "Dad, did you know that it was going to be like this?"
He smirked and said, "Yep." I remember thinking, "Huh?"
Maybe this is what my family and I were meant for—being
Jesus' hands and feet, no matter where that was.

But honestly, I was afraid to go home. I felt like it was so
much easier to follow Jesus in Haiti than it was back in my
hometown. I knew the life I left would be calling me back.

The Point of Discipline

When I (Brock still) was about 12 years old, I remember my
dad letting me in on a secret once when I was in trouble. He
said, "Brock, do you know why I discipline you?" Honestly,
I didn't really know, but I had a few guesses. I would
not have guessed his response though. "I discipline you
because one day I'm going to hand the reins off to you, and
you'll have to discipline yourself. I'm teaching you how to

say no to yourself, and how to say yes to important things. It's just so important that you watch how I do it, because one day soon you'll be in charge of yourself." That made total sense to me. I had an important lesson to learn, I was going to be in charge of my life for the rest of my life, and I needed some important tools to make it to true manhood.

Remember the VW that I (Marko) totaled a week after getting my driver's license? My dad had, earlier that day, placed an ad in the paper to sell that car. (Remember when we sold things in the classifieds section?) On the long drive home from that date, my dad said exactly and only one thing to me: "That was the most expensive date you'll ever have." He made me buy the car from him, at his full asking price. I had to learn how to get the heap towed and sold for scrap. He asked me to suggest a payment plan, which he approved, and for the next year, I made payments for a car I didn't have. But here's the zinger: I *knew*—even at that time—that he was right. I might not have liked it, but I was watching and learning.

His Voice Matters

For many guys, their main questions in life are, "Do I measure up? Am I strong enough, smart enough, and funny enough? Do I fit in?" These questions start early. Remember your son's first day of kindergarten? You dropped off an innocent, cute, and naïve boy only to pick up a brilliantly snarky, line-crossing, one-upper son—especially when you saw him around his friends.

There's a longing deep within guys to fit in, to measure up, and to fully belong and contribute to the "club" of men. If you listen you will hear them say (even if they don't use these words), "I long to find a place where people know me, where people care about me, as me! Don't you understand that I need to fit in and feel like I am good enough?" As parents we need to help them see how they do contribute, how they're gifted, and how they contribute everywhere they go. As parents we can start to meet this longing just by listening, letting him know that his voice matters, and valuing his perspective and skills.

And as he grows into the person he will become, he will develop an emotional resilience. When life gets complicated and the pressure gets intense, when his peers and this culture are pushing him on every side, he will have developed what it takes to live out of his true self, because you will have instilled in him a raw determination to stand and be who he was created to be. As parents, we listen, echo truth back to him, and daily give vision, pointing out how he makes the world a better place.

Developing Emotional Resilience

Emotional resilience is the ability to adapt to stressful situations or crisis. The two greatest fears of students in my town (Brock here; I live in a very affluent bedroom community of New York City) are the fear of peer rejection and the fear of academic failure. Because of this intense perceived pressure, the party scene with sex, drugs, and alcohol are way out of control. Not many of the teenagers have emotional resilience, so when the pressure is high and the heat is on, they simply choose to turn their brains off.

Someone with resilience (our hope for your son and *our own* teenagers!) looks like this: In the midst of a difficult situation, they continue to have perspective, optimism, a sense of humor, spirituality, and a high degree of perseverance. Life might be wonderful, but we all know that difficulty can be just around the corner. We all long for our guys to have the character to withstand and actually grow in the midst of tough times, but how do we help them?

First, guys who are developing into resilient people have learned how to self-talk. They've had adults help them learn to face challenges head-on and speak positively to themselves. Resilient people never respond to challenges in fear, self-pity, or with a blaming mentality.

Second, emotionally resilient people are self-actualized. This is a tall order for teenage guys who are still figuring out who they are. But the hope of emotionally and relationally engaged parents everywhere is that their sons will at least have a strong sense of "this is who I am at this point in time, even though I'm still growing and changing." This means we want our sons to know why they feel what they feel or why they do what they do. Basically, we want them to know themselves. Knowing why a guy feels upset can provide valuable information about what needs to change in his life.

Third, it's important to learn how to surround yourself with and live life in community. Emotionally resilient people have learned how to get people to rally with them. They don't go inward and hide or withdraw when tough times come. They have learned that life's challenges are best faced with deep-spirited friends. This is a huge reason why we've challenged you to be intentional about *curating* strong and positive friendships for your son.

Finally, the word *resilient* means that you just don't give up. You keep going; you persevere. This is what we want our guys to do, right? We want them to become men who fight for what is right in the midst of life's most difficult challenges.

CHAPTER 4: PARENTING STYLES

As youth workers, we see the effects of all types of parenting. We can usually tell within the first five minutes of meeting a teenager what kind of home he or she comes from. It really is amazing, whether we know it or not, how much impact parents have. Unfortunately, if we're not careful, we become taxi drivers instead of parents, chaperones instead of shepherds, and rule makers instead of mentors. There are a lot of ways to parent, but detached, disengaged, dismissive, and permissive shouldn't be anyone's goal as a parent. Rather than go into detail on *unhealthy* approaches to parenting, we're going to use a few pages to unpack some *healthy* ways to approach those years of the adolescent journey.

Parent Friend

I (Brock) remember that when I was about 12 years old, my dad took me out for a drive to hang out. This was a normal thing, the two of us together talking about life. He looked at me and said, "Brock, I want you to know my goal for us over the next few years. The goal is that by the time you're 18, we are close friends." He went on to explain to me the dynamics of this evolving relationship, and that at times it might get confusing. Sometimes he would have to put his foot down, but over the next few years he would be handing the reins of authority to me. It sounded good to me because I loved my dad and he was the type of guy I'd love to be friends with. Over the next few years, we lived a wonderful and difficult journey as my dad let the reins out, then at times pulled them back in, followed by relaxing the reins again. We'd go have a catch in the yard, go play golf, shoot baskets in the driveway, and wash the car, but then we would have talks about this difficult journey. By the time I was 18, my dad and I had made the transition to being deep-spirited friends.

My (Marko) journey to friendship with my father took a few years longer than Brock's, probably because I was still deep into the process of figuring out who I was well into my 20s. But by the time I was about 21 or 22, it was clear that my dad was my friend. And there's no question that, more than 25 years later, our friendship is extremely valuable both to my dad and to me.

Guide and Visionary

Another vision for parenting is to be a guide and a visionary. When training youth workers, we often tell them that their role is to be "tour guides" on the adolescent experience. But remember, you'll have *way* more impact on the life of your son (for good or ill!) than any other adult. You are the "lead tour guide!"

You may have noticed that we talked about the idea of curating in a previous paragraph. At a museum, of course, the curator is the person who decides what art gets displayed. This person manages the collection of art and puts together experiences for the patrons and visitors. In many ways, the best parents for teenage guys act as curators. You have a broader perspective on life and a broader set of experiences. Your role is to be intentional about highlighting: identifying and nurturing competencies in your son, pointing out excesses and lies in culture, and pointing the spotlights toward Jesus and the fullness of a life following him.

Player-Manager

The manager on a baseball team chooses the batting order and the starting lineup, and then makes substitutions throughout the game. Some managers control everything from the pitch selection to decisions to bunt, steal, or pitch out. Other managers will empower players to determine the best strategy on the field. But then there's that rare player-manager. Frank Robinson is a hero and one of the greatest baseball players of all time. During the last two years of his career, he was not only the best player on his team, but he also managed the whole club. Not only was this completely unusual at the time, but in doing so he became the first African-American manager in Major League Baseball history.

Player-managers are engaged, strategic, and deeply part of the game. They get the players prepared and ready to compete, and then they trust each one of them to play. But most importantly, they are right there with them on the field. They are not disengaged, sitting in the dugout, sucking on sunflower seeds. There is a posture of humility and an "I'm one of you" attitude, yet they walk with authority.

What a fantastic vision for parenting teenage guys. You are *in the game* with your son! You are still learning, still growing, still figuring out how to follow Jesus daily. You don't pretend to have all the answers, and you don't disengage when challenges arise. You are shoulder-to-shoulder with your son, leading from out in front and encouraging from behind at the same time.

All of the Above

Honestly, if we parents could embody *some* of all three perspectives, what stunning parents we'd be for our teenage sons! We'd be instinctive while leading and guiding and coaching and giving vision to our young men. At times we'd be playing and laughing, while other times we'd give vision, put our foot down, and call them to a better way. We'd be intentionally moving toward friendship and away from control. And we'd be curating the best life. We don't pretend to say this is simple. But as parents, we sure would love to be a friend, a guide and a visionary, with a dash of player-manager. Jesus, help us be that kind of parent!

CHAPTER 5: SETTING THE ATMOSPHERE OF THE HOME

We've talked with thousands of teenage guys about their parents. You would be encouraged to know this: Your son loves you. He might not always show it, but he loves you and he longs for a deep relationship with you. (There are a few exceptions to this, but the parents of those guys wouldn't be reading this book.) Below the surface and the shallowness of being a teenage boy, there is a depth of longings, one of the biggest being the desire for a healthy and loving relationship with you.

Starting Conversations That Dig Deeper

I (Brock) asked one 16-year-old boy what he talked about with his parents. He said, "Nothing really. They just ask me if I got my homework done and when I need to be picked up from school tomorrow. That's about the extent of it." I asked if he was happy with that. His response? "Yeah, I guess; it's just how it is." Then he thought a second and said, "Actually no, I hate it!"

Consider this: Once a week, take your son on a date. Go get some coffee or a soft drink and talk. At first, it might be awkward, but keep doing it. Ask him about his friends. Ask him about how he really is doing. Ask what makes him angry. And ask what he loves. Then when he answers say this: "Tell me more about that." Then when he tells you more say, "Oh wow, tell me more!" Before long, you will learn where your son's heart is, and he will learn how to dig deep and find out what is really going on inside of himself.

Setting Rules Together

In the midst of our busy lives, don't forget to set reasonable boundaries and have consequences when lines are crossed. Together decide what the rules should be, and together come up with the consequences. If chores aren't done, your son needs to know in advance what the consequences will be. If he misses curfew, make sure you've already agreed what the consequence for that will be. This approach keeps things from heating up and gives your son more ownership of the atmosphere in the home. And please, don't remove consequences (as we see *so many* parents do)! Removing consequences actually does damage to your son.

Setting Him Free

Ultimately we are called to set our sons free. Freedom is about liberation—liberation from the tyranny of the false self. Good parents have been cultivating self-discipline, integrity, and an active faith in their son since the day he was born. That's really the goal, isn't it? That he gets a vision to live big and wide-open, following Jesus to places most aren't willing to go? Of course, when you set him free and he leaves your home, your role as parent doesn't end. He will need your continued care and advice. I (Marko) find that I'm *much more* interested in my dad's advice today than when I was 16!

CHAPTER 6: HOW TO RUIN A LIFE

I (Brock) sat with a group seven high school guys one afternoon at a coffee shop. We were talking girls, sports, and high school life. Then one of them asked me how I got into youth ministry. I told them how God calls us to places and to people. And how when I was 18 years old, God made it clear what I was supposed to do with my life. I looked at them and said, "You know, God ruined my life. I had a plan and God messed it all up."

They seemed a little unsure how to respond to that, but then I added, "My prayer is that God ruins *your* plans for your life. His dreams for you are way cooler." They got it; they understood. We went on to talk about how God's plans are so much bigger than our own plans. My plan was to be a P.E. teacher and to play dodgeball for the rest of my life. God's plan was so much more dynamic than my own. And as a youth pastor, I still get to play dodgeball!

As we write this, we are praying that God ruins your son's life. We're praying that your son runs into Jesus and finds that God has been dreaming about him since before your boy was even born. We pray that your son's eyes are open to a better way, a way of life that is often the polar opposite from the values of our culture and the world he's been living in. We pray that God wakes him up to the reality of the way of Jesus and how Jesus' lordship is so good.

A few weeks ago I (Brock) was with some of those same coffee shop guys on a mission trip when one of them came up to me and said with a smirk, "Brock, God has ruined my life! I think he's calling me to the mission field." Ruined? *Check.*

I remember one Saturday afternoon my dad popped into my room. I must have been about 12 or 13 years old. He said, "Brock, I've got to read this to you!" "OK? What?" He said, "It's in 2 Corinthians and it's amazing!" I thought, "Amazing? Something in the Bible is amazing? OK." Then he read it to me:

Are they servants of Christ? (I am out of my mind to talk like this.) I am more. I have worked much harder, been in prison more frequently, been flogged more severely, and been exposed to death again and again. Five times I received from the Jews the forty lashes minus one. Three times I was beaten with rods, once I was pelted with stones, three times I was shipwrecked, I spent a night and a day in the open sea, I have been constantly on the move. I have been in danger from rivers, in danger from bandits, in danger from my fellow Jews, in danger from Gentiles; in danger in the city, in danger in the country, in danger at sea; and in danger from false believers. I have labored and toiled and have often gone without sleep; I have known hunger and thirst and have often gone without food; I have been cold and naked. Besides everything else, I face daily the pressure of my concern for all the churches (2 Corinthians 11:23-28 NIV).

My dad finished reading and said, excitedly, "What adventure Paul had in following Jesus, huh?" Then he just kind of skipped out of the room leaving me there speechless.

I kind of chuckled and went back to playing my Atari®. But it hit me about 15 minutes later. See, I had begun to think that following Jesus was about *not* doing certain things. For me the gospel was about sin management, not an adventurously expectant life. But as a kid, I wanted an adventurous, expectant life. Since the time I was little I had imagined myself being chased by bandits and lost at sea and doing dangerous things, all for the mission that I was on. And now my dad read me something that really resonated. For the first time in my life, I thought that maybe God was calling me into a life of adventure.

How we see and define ourselves is so vital. This understanding can direct our future more than anything else in life. For guys, we tend to define ourselves by what we do and by what we're good at. We can also define ourselves by our failures and our shortcomings as well. Either direction is dangerous. Instead, we need to catch a vision for an adventurous, expectant life, and allow that sense of calling and vision to define who we are.

We don't know how your son sees himself. Our best guess would be that he defines himself by what he's good at, or by what he's not good at. But you need to know something: He's going to be told who he is every day. His friends will tell him who is, TV and other media will try to define him, his successes and failures will try to box him in and label him. But as a parent, you have a *more important* voice. You can tell your son who he *really* is, and even if it seems like he's not listening, your words will find traction.

Pray that you would see your son with God's eyes, because you've got to carry that vision to your teenage guy. It's so important that you tell him who he really is every day. This will be key in seeing him join the movement toward God-honoring manhood.

One evening after youth group, my mom came up to me (Brock) and said, "I saw you during the worship and singing time at youth group tonight." I thought, "Oh no!" I was that kid in the back row goofing off, making fart noises, and distracting an entire section of kids. But then she said, "Brock, when you worship, it's just so beautiful. When you sing to the Lord, I can tell how much you love him." *Whaaat?* She went on, "When you worship, it so encourages me."

I walked away thinking my mom must have been *on* something. But the funny thing is, my mom's words gave me vision. I found out years later that she had been praying that God would give her eyes to see my true heart. It's just so crazy because her words completely tricked me. The following week at youth group, the vision she had cast just haunted me. I found that for the first time, I was looking at the lyrics. I started to authentically sing these prayers to God. I found myself doing something that I never thought I would do. Months later I started to discover that I was falling in love with Jesus.

Raising a teenage guy to be a God-honoring man is no easy task. It's complex and dynamic, and it requires a lifetime of investment. But God wants to give you insight into your son. God wants to inspire you to be creative and thoughtful. God is going to use you—is *already* using you—in amazing ways. And God is getting ready to wonderfully ruin your son's life. Amen to that!

Check out all the books in our
PARENT'S GUIDE Series!